I0158619

POETRY FROM CRESCENT
MOON

Walking In Cornwall
by Ursula Le Guin

Hymns To the Night
by Novalis

*Hymns To the Night: In
Translation*
by Novalis

*Flower Pollen: Selected
Thoughts*
by Novalis

*Novalis: His Life, Thoughts
and Works*
by Novalis

Edmund Spenser: *Heavenly
Love: Selected Poems*
selected and introduced by
Teresa Page

Edmund Spenser: *Amoretti*
edited by Teresa Page

*The Visions of Petrarch and
Bellay: Early Sonnets*
by Edmund Spenser

Percy Bysshe Shelley:
*Paradise of Golden Lights:
Selected Poems*
selected and introduced by
Charlotte Greene

Robert Herrick: *Delight In
Disorder: Selected Poems*
edited and introduced by
M.K. Pace

Robert Herrick: *Hesperides*
edited and introduced by
M.K. Pace

Robert Herrick: *Upon Julia's
Breasts: Love Poems*
edited and introduced by
M.K. Pace

Sir Thomas Wyatt: *Love For
Love: Selected Poems*
selected and introduced by
Louise Cooper

John Donne: *Air and Angels:
Selected Poems*
selected and introduced by
A.H. Ninham

D.H. Lawrence: *Being Alive:
Selected Poems*
edited with an introduction by
Margaret Elvy

D.H. Lawrence: *Amores*
edited with an introduction by
Margaret Elvy

D.H. Lawrence: *Look! We
Have Come Through!*
edited with an introduction by
Margaret Elvy

D.H. Lawrence: *Love Poems and Others*
edited with an introduction by Margaret Elvy

D.H. Lawrence: *New Poems*
edited with an introduction by Margaret Elvy

D.H. Lawrence: Symbolic Landscapes
by Jane Foster

D.H. Lawrence: Infinite Sensual Violence
by M.K. Pace

Thomas Hardy: *Her Haunting Ground: Selected Poems*
edited, with an introduction by A.H. Ninham

Thomas Hardy: *Late Lyrics and Earlier*
edited, with an introduction by A.H. Ninham

Thomas Hardy: *Moments of Vision*
edited, with an introduction by A.H. Ninham

Thomas Hardy: *Poems of the Past and the Present*
edited, with an introduction by A.H. Ninham

Thomas Hardy: *Satires of Circumstance*
edited, with an introduction by A.H. Ninham

Thomas Hardy: *Time's Laughingstocks*
edited, with an introduction by A.H. Ninham

Thomas Hardy: *Wessex Poems*
edited, with an introduction by A.H. Ninham

Sexing Hardy: Thomas Hardy and Feminism
by Margaret Elvy

Emily Bronte: *Darkness and Glory: Selected Poems*
selected and introduced by Miriam Chalk

John Keats: *Bright Star: Selected Poems*
edited with an introduction by Miriam Chalk

John Keats: *Poems of 1820*
edited with an introduction by Miriam Chalk

Henry Vaughan: *A Great Ring of Pure and Endless Light: Selected Poems*
selected and introduced by A.H. Ninham

The Crescent Moon Book
of Nature Poetry

The Crescent Moon Book
of Nature Poetry

From Langland To Lawrence

Edited by Margaret Elvy

CRESCENT MOON

CRESCENT MOON PUBLISHING
P.O. Box 1312, Maidstone
Kent, ME14 5XU, Great Britain
www.crmoon.com

First published 1994. Second edition 2008. Third edition 2016.
Pocket edition 2022. Introduction © Margaret Elvy, 1994, 2008,
2016, 2022.

Set in Times New Roman.
Designed by Radiance Graphics.

British Library Cataloguing in Publication data

The Crescent Moon Book of Nature Poetry: From Langland to
Lawrence
– (British Poets Series)
1. Nature Poetry
I. Elvy, Margaret II. Book of Nature Poetry II. Nature Poetry
821.008036

ISBN-13 9781861711328
ISBN-13 9781861718495

CONTENTS

ANONYMOUS
(13th century)

["Sumer is y-cumen in"]

SUMER IS y-cumen in,
    Lude sing, cuccu!
Groweth sed and bloweth med
    And springeth the wude nu.
       Sing, cuccu!
Awe belteth after lamb,
    Lowth after calve cu;
Bulluc sterteth, bucke ferteth.
    Merie sing, cuccu!
       Cuccu, cuccu,
Wel singes thu, cuccu;
Ne swik thu never nu!

Sing, cuccu, nu! Sing cuccu!
Sing, cuccu! Sing, cuccu, nu!

ANONYMOUS
(13th century)

Spring

LENTEN IS come with love to towne,
With blosmen and with briddes rowne,
    That al this blisse bringeth;
Dayeseyes in thes dales,
Notes swete of nightegales –
    Ech fowl song singeth.
The threstecok him threteth o,
Away is here winter wo,
    When woderove springeth.
Thes fowles singeth ferly fele,
And wliteth on here winne wele,
    That al the wode ringeth.

The rose raileth hire rode,
The leves on the lighte wode
    Waxen al with wille.
The moone mandeth hire blee,
The lilie is lofsom to see,
    The fenil and the fille.
Wawes these wilde drakes;

✳ 16

Miles murgeth here makes,
    As strem that striketh stille.
Mody meneth, so doth mo –
Ich' ot ich am one of tho
    For love that likes ille.

The moone mandeth hire light;
So doth the seemly sunne bright,
    When briddes singeth breme.
Dewes donketh the downes;
Deeres with her derne rownes,
    Domes for to deme;
Wormes woweth under cloude;
Wimmen waxeth wonder proude –
    So wel it wil hem seme.
If me shal wante wille of on,
This winne wele I wil forgon,
    And wight in wode be fleme.

WILLIAM LANGLAND
(1330s-1400?))

from *The Field Full of Folk*

IN SOMER seson whenne softe was the sunne
I shop me into a shroud as I a shep were,
In habite as an hermite unholy of werkes,
Wente wide in this world wondres to here.
But on a May morwening upon malerne hills
Me befel a ferly, of fairye me thoughte;
I was wery ofwandred and wente me to reste
Under a brod bank by a bournes side;
And as I lay and lenede and lookede on the watres,
I slomerede into a sleeping, it swyede so merye,
Thenne gan I mete a merveillous swevene:
That I was in a wildernesse, wiste I nevere where;
Ac as I beheld into the Est on high to the sunne
I saw a towr on a toft tryely y-maked;
A deep dale benethe, a daungeoun thereinne
With deepe dikes and derke and dredful of sight.
    A fair feeld ful of folk fand I there-betweene,
Of alle maner of men, the mene and the riche,
Worching and wandringe as the world asketh.
Some pure hem to plow, playede ful selde,

In setting and sowing swunke ful harde,
Wonne that these wastours with glotonye destroyeth.

GEOFFREY CHAUCER
(1340?-1400)

["Now welcome, somer"]

NOW WELCOME, somer, with thy sunne softe,
That hast thes wintres wedres overshake
And driven away the longe nightes blake!

Saint Valentin, that art ful hy o-lofte,
Thus singen amale fowles for thy sake:
    'now welcome, somer, with thy sunne softe,
    that hast thes wintres wedres overshake!'

Wel han they cause for to gladden ofte,
Sith ech of hem recovered hath his make;
Ful blissful mowe they singe when they wake:
    'Now welcome, somer, with thy sunne softe,
    That hast thes wintres wedres overshake
    And driven away the longe nightes blake!'

SIR THOMAS WYATT
(1503-1542)

(attributed)

["I must go walk the woods so wild"]

I MUST go walk the woods so wild
    And wander here and there
    In dread and deadly fear,
For where I trust,
 I am beguiled
    And all for your love, my dear.

I am banished from my bliss
    By craft and false pretence,
    Faultless, without offence;
And of return no certain is
    And all for your love, my dear.

Banished am I, remedies,
    To wilderness alone,
    Alone to sigh and moan
And of relief all comfortless
    And all for your love, my dear.

My house shall be the greenwood tree,
    A tuft of brakes my bed.
    And this my life I lead
As one that from his joy doth flee
    And all for your love, my dear.

The running streams shall be my drink.
    Acorns shall be my food.
    Naught else shall do me good
But on your beauty for to think
    And all for your love, my dear.

And when the deer draw to the green,
    Makes me think on a roe:
    How I have seen ye go
Above the fairest, fairest be seen!
    And all for your love, my dear.

But where I see in any coast
    Two turtles sit and play,
    Rejoicing all the day,
Alas, I think, this have I lost
    And all for your love, my dear.

No bird, no bush, no bough I see
    But bringeth to my mind
    Something whereby I find
My heart far wandered, far from me,

And all for your love, my dear.

The tune of birds when I do hear,
    My heart doth bleed, alas,
    Remembering how I was
Wont for to hear your ways so clear
    And all for your love, my dear.

My thought doth please me for the while:
    While I see my desire
    Naught else I do require.
So with my thought I me beguile
    And all for your love, my dear.

Yet I am further from my thought
    Than earth from heaven above.
    And yet for to remove
My pain, alas, availeth naught
    And all for your love, my dear.

And where I lie, secret, alone,
    I mark that face anon
    That stayeth my life, as one
That other comfort can get none
    And all for your love, my dear.

The summer days that be so long
    I walk and wander wide,

Alone, without a guide,
Always thinking how I have wrong
    And all for your love, my dear.

The winter nights that are so cold
    I lie amid the [storms],
    Unwrapped, in particular thorns,
Remembering my sorrows old
    And all for your love, my dear.

A woeful man such desert life
    Becometh best of all.
    But woe might them befall
That are the causers of this strife
    And all for your love, my dear.

SIR WALTER RALEIGH
(*c*.1552-1618)

The Nymph's Reply to the Sheepheard

IF ALL the world and love were young,
And truth in every Sheepheards tongue,
These pretty pleasures might me move,
To live with thee, and be thy love.

Time drives the flocks from field to fold,
When Rivers rage, and rocks grow cold,
And Philomell becommeth dombe,
The rest complaines of cares to come.

The flowers doe fade, and wanton fieldes,
To wayward winter reckoning yeeldes,
A honny tongue, a hart of gall,
Is fancies spring, but sorrowes fall.

Thy gownes, thy shooes, thy beds of Roses,
Thy cap, thy kirtle, and thy poesies,
Soone breake, soone wither, soone forgotten:
In follie ripe, in reason rotten.

Thy belt of straw and ivie buddes,
Thy Corall claspes and Amber studdes,
All these in me no meanes can move,
To come to thee, and be the love.

But could youth last, and love still breede,
Had joyes no date, nor age no neede,
Then these delights my minde might move,
To live with thee, and by thy love.

SIR PHILIP SIDNEY
(1554-1586)

from *The Countess of Pembroke's Arcadia*

O SWEET woods, the delight of solitariness,
O how much I do like your solitariness!
Where man's mind hath a freed consideration
Of goodness to receive lovely direction;
Where senses do behold th' order of heavenly host,
And wise thoughts do behold what the creator is.
Contemplation here holdeth his only seat,
Bounded with no limits, borne with a wing of hope,
Climbs even unto the stars; Nature is under it.
Nought disturbs thy quiet; all to thy service yield;
Each sight draws on a thought, thought mother of
                                    science;
Sweet birds kindly do grant harmony unto thee;
Fair trees' shade is enough fortfication,
Nor danger to thyself if be not in thyself.

O sweet words, the delight of solitariness,
O how much I do like your solitariness!
Here no treason is hid, veiled in innocence,
Nor envy's snaky eye finds any harbour here,

Nor flatterers' venomous insinuations,
Nor cunning humorists' puddled opinions,
Nor courteous ruin of proffered usury,
Nor time prattled away, cradle of ignorance,
Nor causeless duty, nor cumber of arrogance,
Nor trifling title of vanity dazzleth us,
Nor golden manacles stand for a paradise.
Here wrong's name is unheard; slander a monster is.
Keep thy spirit from abuse, here no abuse doth haunt.
What man grafts in a tree dissimulation?

O sweet woods, the delight of solitariness,
O how well I do like your solitariness!
Yet dear soil, if a soul closed in a mansion
As sweet as violets, fair as a lily is,
Straight as a cedar, a voice stains the canary birds,
Whose shade safety doth hold, danger avoideth her;
Such wisdom, that in her lives speculation;
Such goodness, that in her simplicity triumphs;
Where envy's snaky eye winketh or else dieth;
Slander wants a pretext, flattery gone beyond;
O, if such a one have bent a lonely life
Her steps, glad we receive, glad we receive her eyes,
And think not she doth hurt our solitariness:
For such company decks our solitariness.

SAMUEL DANIEL
(1562-1619)

from *Delia*

BUT LOVE whilst that thou mayst be loved again,
    Now whilst thy May hath filled thy lap with flowers,
Now whilst thy beauty without a stain;
    Now use thy summer miles ere winter lours.
And whilst thou spread'st unto the rising sun
    The fairest flower that ever saw the light,
Now joy thy time before thy sweet be done:
    And, Delia, think thy morning must have night,
And what thy brightness sets at length to west,
    When thou wilt close up that which now thou
                    showest;
And think the same becomes thy fading best,
    Which then shall hide it most and cover lowest.
        Men do not weigh the stalk for that it was,
        When once they find her flower, her glory, pass.

MICHAEL DRAYTON
(1563-1631)

from *Idea, The Shepheardes Garland*

The First Eglog

NOW *PHOEBUS* from the equinoctiall Zone,
Had task'd his teame unto the higher sphere,
And from the brightness of his glorious throne,
Sends forth his Beams to light the lower ayre,
The cheerful welkin, comen this long look'd hower,
Distils adowne full many a silver shower.

Fayre *Philomel* night-musicke of the spring,
Sweetly records her tuneful harmony,
And with deep sobbes, and doleful sorrowing,
Before fayre *Cinthya* actes her Tragedy:
The Throstlecock, by breaking of the day,
Chants to his sweete, full many a lovely lay.

The crawling snake, against the morning sunne,
Now streaks him in his rayn-bow coloured cote:
The darkesome shades, as loathsome he doth shunne,
Inchanted with the Birds sweete silvan note:

The Buck forsakes the lands where he hath fed,
And scorns the hunt should view his velvet head.

Through all the parts, dispersed is the blood,
The lustie spring, in flower of all her pride,
Man, bird, and beast, and fish, in pleasant flood,
Rejoicing all in this most joyful tide:
Save *Rowland* leaning on a Ranpick tree,
O'r grown with age, forlorn with woe was he.

Oh blessed *Pan*, tho shepheards god sayth he,
O thou Creator of the starrie light,
Whose wonderous works shew thy divinitie,
Thou wise inventor of the day and night,
Refreshing nature with the lovely spring,
Quite blemisht erst, with stormy winters sting.

O thou strong builder of the firmament,
Who placedst *Phoebus* in his fierie Carre,
And by thy mighty Godhead didst invent,
The planets mansions that they should not jarre,
Orderyning *Phoebe*, mistress of the night,
From *Tytans* flame to steal her forked light.

Even from the clearest christall shining throne,
Under whose feet the heavens are low abased,
Commanding in thy majestie alone,
Whereas the fiery Cherubines are placed:

Receive my vows as incense unto thee,
My tribute due to thy eternitie.

O shepheards soveraigne, yea receive in green,
The gushing tears, from never-resting eyes,
And let those prayers which I shall make to thee,
Be in thy sight perfumed sacrifice:
Let smokie sighs be pledges of contrition,
For follies past to make my souls submission.

Submission makes amends for all my misse,
Contrition a refined life begins,
Then sacred sighs, what thing more precious is?
And prayers be oblations for my sinnes,
Repentant tears, from heaven-beholding eyes,
Ascend the ayre, and penetrate the skies.

My sorrows wax, my joys are in the wayning,
My hopes decayes, and my despayre is springing,
My love hath loss, and my disgrace hath gayning,
Wrong rules, desert with tears her hands sits wringing:
Sorrow, despayre, disgrace, and wrong, do thwart
My Joy, my love, my hope, and my desert.

Devouring time shall swallow up my sorrows,
And strong belief shall torture black despair,
Death shall orewhelme disgrace, in deepest furrows,
And Justice laie my wrongs upon the Beere:

Thus Justice, death, belief, and time, ere long,
Shall end my woes, despayre, disgrace, and wrong.

Yet time shall be expir'd and lose his date,
And full assurance cancel strongest trust,
Eternitie shall trample on deathes pate,
And Justice shall surcease when all be just:
Thus time, belief, death, Justice, shall surcease,
By date, assurance, eternity, and peace.

Thus breathing from the Centre of his soule,
The tragick accents of his extasie,
His sun-set eyes gan here and there to roule,
Like one surprisde with sodaine lunacie:
And being rouzde out of melancholy,
Fly whirle-winde thoughts unto the heavens quoth he.

Now in the Ocean *Tytan* quencht his flame,
And summond *Cinthya* to set up her light,
The heavens with their glorious starry frame,
Preparde to crowne the sable-vayled night:
When *Rowland* from this time-consumed stock,
With stone-colde hart now stalketh towards his flock.

WILLIAM SHAKESPEARE
(1564-1616)

["I would I had some flowers o' the spring that might"]

I WOULD I had some flowers o' the spring that might
Become your time of day; and yours, and yours,
That wear upon your virgin branches yet
Your maidenheads growing: O Prosperina!
For the flowers now that frighted me thou let'st fall
From Dis's waggon! – daffodils,
That come before the swallow dares, and take
The winds of March with beauty; violets, dim
But sweeter than the lids of Juno's eyes
Or Cytherea's breath; pale primroses,
That die unmarried ere they can behold
Bright Phoebus in his strength – a malady
Most incident to maids; bold oxlips, and
The crown-imperial; lilies of all kinds,
The flow'r-de-luce being one. O, these I lack
To make you garlands of, and my sweet friend
To strew him him o'er and o'er!

Perdita. *The Winter's Tale*, 4.4.113-128

["Blow, winds, and crack your cheeks; rage, blow"]

BLOW, WINDS, and crack your cheeks; rage, blow.
You cataracts and hurricanoes, spout
Till you have drench'd our steeples, drown'd the cocks.
You sulph'rous and thought-executing fires,
Vaunt-couriers of oak-chewing thunder-bolts,
Singe my white head. And thou, all-shaking thunder,
Strike flat the thick rotundity o' th' world;
Crack nature's moulds, all germens spill at once,
That makes ingrateful man.
[...]
Rumble thy bellyful. Spit, fire; spout, rain.
Nor rain, wind, thunder, fire, are my daughters.
I tax not your elements, with unkindness;
I never gave you kingdom, call'd you children;
You owe me no subscription. Then let fall
Your horrible pleasure. Here I stand, your slave,
A poor, infirm, weak and despis'd old man;
But yet I call you servile ministers
That will with two pernicious daughters join
Your high-engender'd battles 'gainst a head
So old and white as this. O ho! 'tis foul!

Lear. *King Lear*, 3.2.1-9, 14-25

Ye elves of hills, brooks, standing lakes, and groves;
And ye that on the sands with printless foot
Do chase the ebbing Neptune, and do fly him
When he comes back; you demi-puppets that
By moonshine do the green sour ringlets make,
Whereof the ewe not bites; and you whose pastime
Is to make midnight mushrooms, that rejoice
To hear the solemn curfew; by whose aid –
Weak masters though ye be – I have bedimm'd
The noontide sun, call'd forth the mutinous winds,
And 'twixt the green sea and the azur'd vault
Set roaring war. To the dread rattling thunder
Have I given fire, and rifted Jove's stout oak
With his own bolt; the strong-bas'd promontory
Have I made shake, and by the spurs pluck'd up
The pine and cedar. Graves at my command
Have wak'd their sleepers, op'd, and let 'em forth,
By my so potent art. But this rough magic
I here abjure; and, when I have requir'd
Some heavenly music – which even now I do –
To work mine end upon their senses that
This airy charm is for, I'll break my staff,
Bury it certain fathoms in the earth,
And deeper than did ever plummet sound
I'll drown my book.

Prospero. *The Tempest*, 5.1.33-57

ROBERT HERRICK
(1591-1674)

The Argument of His Book

I SING of Brooks, *of* Blossomes, Birds, *and* Bowers:
Of April, May, *of* June, *and* July-Flowers.
I sing of May-poles, Hock-carts, Wassails, Wakes,
Of Bride-grooms, Brides, *and of their* Bridall-cakes.
I write of Youth, *of* Love, *and have Accesse*
*By these, to sing of cleanly-*Wantonnesse.
I sing of Dewes, *of* Raines, *and piece by piece*
Of Balme, *of* Oyle, *of* Spice, *and* Amber-gris.
I sing of Times trans-shifting; *and I write*
How Roses *first came* Red, *and* Lillies White.
I write of Groves, *of* Twilights, *and I sing*
The Court of Mab, *and of the* Fairie-King.
I write of Hell; *I sing (and ever shall)*
Of Heaven, *and hope to have it after all.*

To Meddowes

YE HAVE been fresh and green,
    Ye have been fill'd with flower:
And ye the Walks have been
    Where Maids have spent their houres.

You have beheld, how they
    With *Wicker Arks* did come
To kisse, and beare away
    The richer Couslips home.

Y'ave heard them sweetly sing,
    And seen them in a Round:
Each Virgin, like a Spring,
    With Hony-succles crown'd.

But now, we see, none here,
    Whose silv'rie feet did tread,
And with dishevell'd Haire,
    Adorn'd this smoother mead.

Like Unthrifts, having spent,
    Your stock, and needy grown,
Y'are left here to lament
    Your poore estates, alone.

FAIRE PLEDGES of a fruitful Tree,
    Why do ye fall so fast?
    Your date is not so past;
But you may stay yet here a while,
    To blush and gently smile;
        And go at last.

What, were ye borne to be
    An hour or half's delight;
    And so to bid goodnight?
'Twas pitie Nature brought ye forth
    Merely to show your worth,
        And lose you quite.

But you are lovely Leaves, where we
    May read how soon things have
    Their end, though ne'er so brave:
And after they have shown their pride,
    Like you a while: they Glide
        Into the Grave.

The Succession of the Four Sweet Months

First, *April*, she with mellow showers
Opens the way for early flowers;
Then after her comes smiling *May*,
In a more rich and sweet array:
Next enters *June*, and brings us more
Jems, then those two, that went before:
Then (lastly) *July* comes, and she
More wealth brings in, then all those three.

Cherry Ripe

Cherry-ripe, ripe, ripe, I cry,
Full and fair ones; come, and buy:
If so be you ask me where
They do grow? I answer, there
Where my Julia's lips do smile; –
There's the land, or cherry-isle;
Whose plantations fully show
All the year where cherries grow.

HENRY VAUGHAN
(1621-1695)

A Fluvium Iscam

ISCA PARENS florum, placido qui spumens ore
     Lambis lapillos aureos,
Qui mæstos hyacinthos, et picti tophi
     Mulces susurris humidis,
Dumque novas *pergunt* menses *consumere* lunas
     Coelumque mortales *terit,*
Accumulas cum sole *dies, ævumque per omne*
     Fidelis *induras* latex,
O quis inaccessos et quali murmure lucos
     Mutumque *solaris* nemus!
Per te discerpti credo Thracis *ire querelas*
Plectrumque divini sensis.

To the River Usk

USK, FATHER of flowers, foaming from your quiet
spring, you lap the golden pebbles, and with your moist
murmurings soothe the sorrowful hyacinths and the flora
on the colourful rock; and while the months run on to
engulf new moons, and heaven wears down mortal men,
you number your days with the sun, and last out every
age, an unfailing stream. What comfort you bring to the
remote woods and the silent grove, and with what a
murmurous whisper! I believe that the plaints of the
dismembered Thracian move along your waters, and the
lyre of the divine old man.

Regeneration

1

A WORD, and still in bonds, one day
        I stole abroad,
It was high-spring, and all the way
      Primrosed, and hung with shade;
      Yet, was it frost within,
        And surly winds
Blasted my infant buds, and sin
      Like clouds eclipsed my mind.

2

Stormed thus, I straight perceived my spring
      Mere stage, and show,
My walk a monstrous, mountained thing
      Rough-cast with rocks, and snow;
      And as a pilgrim's eye
       Far from relief,
Measures the melancholy sky
      Then drops, and rains for grief,

3

So sighed I upwards still; at last
      'Twixt steps, and falls

✲ 44

I reached the pinnacle, where placed
     I found a pair of scales,
     I took them up and laid
        In the one late pains,
The other smoke, and pleasures weighed
        But proved the heavier grains;

4

With that, some cried, Away; straight I
        Obeyed, and led
Full east, a fair, fresh field could spy
        Some called it, Jacob's bed;
        A Virgin-soil, which no
          Rude feet ere trod,
Where (since he stepped there,) only go
        Prophets, and friends of God.

5

Here, I reposed; but scarce well set,
        A grove escried
Of stately height, whose branches met
        And mixed on every side;
        I entered, and once in
          (Amazed to see't,)
Found all was changed, and a new spring
        Did all my senses greet;

6

The unthrift Sun shot vital gold
      A thousand pieces,
And heaven its azure did unfold
      Chequered with snowy fleeces,
      The air was all in spice
      And every bush
A garland wore; thus fed my eyes
      But all the ear lay hush.

7

Only a little fountain lent
      Some use for ears,
And on the dumb shades language spent
      The music of her tears;
      I drew her near, and found
      The cistern full
Of divers stones, some bright, and round
      Others ill-shaped, and dull.

8

The first (pray mark,) as quick as light
      Danced through the flood,
But, the last more heavy than the night
      Nailed to the centre stood;

I wondered much, but tired
        At last with thought,
My restless eye that still desired
    As strange an object brought;

9

It was a bank of flowers, where I descried
        (Though 'twas mid-day,)
Some fast asleep, others broad-eyed
        And taking in the ray,
        Here musing long, I heard
            A rushing wind
Which still increased, but whence it stirred
        No where I could not find;

10

I turned me round, and to each shade
        Dispatched an eye,
To see, if any leaf had made
        Least motion, or reply,
        But while I listening sought
            My mind to ease
By knowing, where 'twas, or where not,
        It whispered; *Where I please*

Lord, then said I, *On me one breath,*
And let me die before my death!

The Morning-Watch

O joys! infinite sweetness! with what flowers,
And shoots of glory, my soul breaks, and buds!
                    All the long hours
                    Of night, and rest
                    Through the still shrouds
                    Of sleep, and clouds,
              This dew fell on my breast;
                    Of how it *blows,*
And *spirits* all my earth! hark! In what rings,
And *hymning circulations* the quick world
                    Awakes, and sings;
                    The rising winds,
                    And falling springs,
                    Birds, beasts, all things
              Adore him in their kinds.
                    Thus all is hurled
In sacred *hymns*, and *order*, the great *chime*
And *symphony* of nature. Prayer is
                    The world in tune,
                    A spirit-voice,
                    And vocal joys
              Whose *echo is* heaven's bliss.
                    O let me climb
When I lie down! The pious soul by night
Is like a clouded star, whose beams though said

To shed their light
Under some cloud
Yet are above,
And shine, and move
Beyond that misty shroud.
So in my bed
That curtained grave, though sleep, like ashes, hide
My lamp, and life, both shall in thee abide.

Peace

My soul, there is a country
    Far beyond the stars,
Where stands a winged sentry
    All skillful in the wars,
There above noise, and danger
    Sweet peace sits crowned with smiles,
And one born in a manger
    Commands the beauteous files,
He is thy gracious friend,
    And (O my soul awake!)
Did in pure love descend
    To die here for thy sake,
If thou canst get but thither,
    There grows the flower of peace,
The rose that cannot wither,
    Thy fortress, and thy ease;
Leave then thy foolish ranges;
    For none can thee secure,
But one, who never changes,
    Thy God, thy life, thy cure.

THOMAS PARNELL
(1679-1717)

from *Heath: An Ecologue*

HERE, WAFTED o'er by mild *Etesian* Air,
Thou Country *Goddess*, beauteous health, repair!
Here let my Breast thro' quivering Trees inhale
Thy rosy Blessing with the Morning Gale.
What are the fields, or Flow'rs, or all I see?
Ah! tasteless all, if not enjoy'd with thee.

Joy to my soul! I feel the *Goddess* nigh,
The Face of Nature cheers as well as I;
O'er the flat Green refreshing Breezes run,
The smiling Dazies blow beneath the sun,
The Brooks run purling down with silver Waves,
The planted Lanes rejoice with dancing leaves,
The chirping Birds from all the Compas rove
To tempt the tuneful Echoes of the Grove:
High sunny Summits, deeply shaded Dales,
Thick Mossy Banks, and flow'ry winding Vales,
With various Prospect gratify the Sight,
And scatter fix'd Attention in Delight.

Come, Country *Goddess*, come; nor thou suffice,
But bring thy mountain-sister, Exercise,
Call'd by thy lively voice, she turns her Pace,
Her winding horn proclaims the finish'd Chace;
She mounts the rocks, she skims the level Plain,
Dogs, Hawks, and Horses, crowd her early Train;
Her hardy Face repels the tanning Wind,
And Lines and meshes loosely float behind,
All these as Means of Toil the Feeble see,
But these are helps to Pleasure join'd with thee.

JAMES THOMSON
(1700-1748)

from *The Seasons: Summer*

BEAR ME, POMONA! to thy citron groves;
To where the lemon and the piercing lime,
With the deep orange glowing through the green,
Their lighter glories blend. Lay me reclined
Beneath the spreading tamarind, that shakes,
Fanned by the breeze, its fever-cooling fruit.
Deep in the night the massy locust sheds
Quench my hot limbs; or lead me through the maze,
Embowering endless, of the Indian fig;
Or, thrown at gayer ease on some fair brow,
Let me behold, by breezy murmur cooled,
Broad o'er my head the verdant cedar wave,
And high palmettos lift their graceful shade.
Oh, stretched amid these orchards of the sun,
Give me to drain the cocoa's milky bowl,
And from the palm to draw its freshening wine!
More bounteous far than all the frantic juice
Which Bacchus pours, nor, on its slender twigs
Low-bending, be the full pomegranate scorned;
Nor, creeping through the woods, the gelid race

Of berries. Oft in humble station dwells
In boastful worth, above fastidious pomp.
Witness, thou best Anana, thou the pride
Of vegetable life, beyond whate'er
The poet's imaged in the golden age:
Quick let me strip thee of thy tufty coat,
Spread thy ambrosial stores, and feast with Jove!
    From these the prospect varies. Plains immense
He stretched below, interminable meads
And vast savannas, where the wandering eye,
Unfixt, is in a verdant ocean lost.
Another Flora there, of bolder hues
And richer sweets beyond our garden's pride,
Plays o'er the fields, and showers with sudden hand
Exuberant spring – for oft these valleys shift
Their green-embroidered robe to fiery brown,
And swift to green again, as scorching suns
Or streaming dews and torrent rains prevail.
Along these lonely regions, where, retired
From little scenes of art, great Nature dwells
In awful solitude, and naught is seen
But the wild herds that own no master's stall,
Prodigious rivers roll their fattening seas;
On whose luxuriant herbage, half-concealed,
Like a fallen cedar, far diffused his train,
Cased in green scales, the crocodile extends.
The flood disparts: behold! in plaited mail
Behemoth rears his head. Glanced from his side,

The darted steel in idle shivers flies:
He fearless walks the plain, or seeks the hills,
Where, as he crops his varied fare, the herds,
In widening circle round, forget their food
And at the harmless stranger wondering gaze.

WILLIAM COLLINS
(1721-1759)

Ode to Evening

IF OUGHT of Oaten Stop, or Pastoral Song,
May hope, chaste Eve, to soothe they modest Ear,
     Like thy own solemn Springs,
     Thy Springs, and dying Gales,
O Nymph reserv'd, while now the bright-hair'd Sun
Sits in yon western Tent, whose cloudy Skirts,
     With Brede ethereal wove,
     O'erhangs his wavy Bed:
Now Air is hush'd, save where the weak-ey'd Bat,
With short shrill Shriek flits by on leathern Wing,
     Or where the Beetle winds
     His small but sullen Horn,
As oft he rises 'midst the twilight Path,
Against the Pilgrim born in heedless hum:
     Now teach me, maid compos'd,
     To breathe some soften'd Strain,
Whose Numbers stealing thro' thy darkening Vale,
May not unseemly with its Stillness suit,
     As musing slow, I hail
     Thy genial lov'd Return!

For when thy folding Star arising shews
His paly Circlet, at his warning Lamp
      The fragrant hours, and Elves
      Who slept in Flow'rs the Day,
And many a Nymph who wreaths her Brows with Sedge,
And sheds the fresh'ning Dew, and lovelier still,
      The pensive Pleasure sweet
      Prepare thy shadowy Car.

Then lead, calm Vot'ress, where some sheety Lake,
Cheers the lone heath, or some time-hallow'd Pile,
      Or up-land Fallow grey
      Reflect its last cool Gleam.
But when chill blust'ring Winds, or driving Rain,
Forbid my willing Feet, be mine the hut,
      That from the mountain's Side,
      Views Wilds, and swelling Floods,
And Hamlets brown, and dim-discover'd Spires,
And hears their simple Bell, and marks o'er all
      The Dewy Fingers draw
      The gradual dusky Veil.

While Spring shall pour his Show'rs, as oft he wont,
And bathe thy breathing Tresses, meekest Eve!
      While Summer loves to sport,
      beneath thy ling'ring Light:
While sallow Autumn fills thy Lap with Leaves,
Or Winter yelling thro' the troublous Air,

Affrights thy shrinking Train,
And rudely rends thy Robes,
So long sure-found beneath thy sylvan Shed,
Shall Fancy, Friendship, Science, rose-lip'd Health,
Thy gentlest Influence own,
And hymn thy fav'rite Name!

MARY LEAPOR
(1722-1746)

from *On Winter*

NOW SHIV'RING Nature mourns her ravished charms,
And sinks supine in winter's frozen arms.
No gaudy banks delight the ravished eye,
But northern breezes whistle through the sky.
No joyful choirs hail the rising day,
But the froze crystal wraps the leafless spray:
Brown look he meadows, that were late so fine,
And capped with ice the distant mountains shine;
The silent linnet views the gloomy sky,
Skulks to his hawthorn, nor attempts to fly:
The heavy clouds send down the feathered snow;
Through naked trees the hollow tempests blow;
The shepherd sighs, but not his sighs prevail;
To the soft snow succeeds the rushing hail'
And these white prospects soon resign their room
To melting showers and unpleasing gloom;
The nymphs and swains their aching fingers blow,
Shun the cold rains and bless the kinder snow;
While the faint travellers around them see,
Here seas of mud and there a leafless tree:

No budding leaves nor honeysuckles gay,
No yellow crow-foots paint the dirty way;
The lark sits mournful as afraid to rise,
And the sad finch his softer song denies.

CHARLOTTE SMITH
(1749-1806)

from *Beachy Head*

AN EARLY worshipper at Nature's shrine,
I loved her rudest scenes – warrens, and heaths,
And yellow commons, and birch-shaded hollows,
And hedge rows, bordering unfrequented lanes
Bowered with wild roses, and the clasping woodbine
Where purple tassels of the tangling vetch
With bittersweet, and bryony inweave,
And the dew fills the silver bindweed's cups –
I loved to trace the brooks whose humid banks
Nourish the harebell, and the freckled pagil;
And stroll among o'ershadowing woods of beech,
Lending in summer, from the heats of noon
A whispering shade; while haply there reclines
Some pensive lover of uncultured flowers,
Who, from the tumps with bright green mosses clad,
Plucks the wood sorrel, with its light thin leaves,
Heart-shaped, and triply folded; and its root
Creeping like beaded coral; or who there
Gathers, the copse's pride, anemones,
With rays like golden studs on ivory laid

Most delicate; but touched with purple clouds,
Fit crown for April's fair but changeful brow.

Ah! hills so early loved! in fancy still
I breathe your pure keen air; and still behold
Those widely spreading views, mocking alike
The poet and the painter's utmost art.

WILLIAM BLAKE
(1757-1827)

Night

THE SUN descending in the west,
The evening star does shine;
The birds are silent in their nest,
And I must seek for mine.
The Moon, like a flower,
In heaven's high bower,
With silent delight
Sits and smiles on the night.

Farewell, green fields and happy groves,
Where flocks have took delight.
Where lambs have nibble, silent moves
The feet of angels bright;
Unseen they pour blessing,
And joy without ceasing,
On each bud and blossom,
And each sleeping bosom.

They look in every thoughtless nest,
Where birds are cover'd warm;

They visit caves of every beast,
To keep them all from harm.
If they see any weeping
That should have been sleeping,
They pour sleep on their head,
And sit down by their bed.
When wolves and tigers howl for prey,
They pitying stand and weep;
Seeking to drive their thirst away,
And keep them from the sheep.
But if they rush dreadful,
The angels, most heedful,
Receive each mild spirit,
New worlds to inherit.

And there the lion's ruddy eyes
Shall flow with tears of gold,
And pitying the tender cries,
And walking round the fold,
Saying: 'Wrath, by His meekness,
And, by His health, sickness
Is driven away.
From our immortal day.

'And now beside thee, bleating lamb,
I can lie down and sleep;
Or think on Him who bore thy name,
Graze after thee and weep.

For, wash'd in life's river,
My bright mane for ever
Shall shine like the gold
As I guard o'er the fold.'

WILLIAM WORDSWORTH
(1770-1850)

from *Lines Composed a Few Miles Above Tintern Abbey*

AND I have felt
A presence that disturbs me with the joy
Of elevated thoughts; a sense sublime
Of something far more deeply interfused,
Whose dwelling is the light of setting suns,
And the round ocean and the living air,
And the blue sky, and in the mind of man:
A motion and a spirit, that impels
All thinking things, all objects of all thought,
And rolls through all things. Therefore am I still
A lover of the meadows and the woods,
And mountains; and of all that we behold
From this green earth; of all the mighty world
Of eye, and ear, – both what they half create,
And what perceive; well pleased to recognize
In nature and the language of the sense,
The anchor of my purest thoughts, the nurse,
The guide, the guardian of my heart, and soul
Of all my moral being.

from *Ode: Intimations of Immortality From
Recollection of Early Childhood*

      O joy! that in our embers
      Is something that doth live,
      That nature yet remembers
      What was so fugitive!
The thought of our past years in me doth breed
Perpetual benediction: not indeed
For that which is most worthy to be blest;
Delight and liberty, the simple creed
Of Childhood, whether busy or at rest,
With new-fledged hope still fluttering in his breast: –
      Not for these I raise
      The song of thanks and praise;
    But for those obstinate questionings
    Of sense and outward things,
    Fallings from us, vanishings;
    Blank misgivings of a Creature
Moving about in worlds not realized,
High instincts before which our mortal Nature
Did tremble like a guilty Thing surprised:
      But for those first affections,
      Those shadowy recollections,
    Which, be they what they may,
Are yet the fountain light of all our day,
Are yet a master light of all our seeing;

Upholds us, cherish, and have power to make
Our noisy years seem moments in the being
Of the eternal Silence: truths that wake,
To perish never;
Which neither listlessness, nor mad endeavour,
Nor Man nor Boy,
Not all that is at enmity with joy,
Can utterly abolish or destroy!
Hence in a season of calm weather
Though inland far we be,
Our Souls have sight of that immortal sea
Which brought us thither,
And see the Children sport upon the shore,
And hear the mighty waters rolling evermore.

Then sing, ye Birds, sing, sing a joyous song!
And let the young Lambs bound
As to the tabor's sound!
We in thought will join your throng,
Ye that pipe and ye that play,
Ye that through your hearts today
Feel the gladness of the May!
What though the radiance which was once so bright
Be now for ever taken from my sight,
Though nothing can bring back the hour
Of splendour in the grass, of glory in the flower;
We will grieve not, rather find
Strength in what remains behind;

In the primal sympathy
Which having been must ever be;
In the soothing thoughts that spring
Out of human suffering;
In the faith that looks through death,
In years that bring the philosophic mind.

And O, ye Fountains, Meadows, Hills, and Groves,
Forbode not any severing of our loves!
Yet in my heart of hearts I feel your might;
I only have relinquished one delight
To live beneath your more habitual sway.
I love the Brooks which down their channels fret,
Even more than when I tripped lightly as they;
The innocent brightness of a new-born Day
         Is lovely yet;
The Clouds that gather round the setting sun
Do take a sober colouring from an eye
That hath kept watch o'er man's mortality;
Another race hath been. And other palms are won.
Thanks to the human heart by which we live,
Thanks to its tenderness, its joys, and fears,
To me the meanest flower that blows can give
Thoughts that do often lie too deep for tears.

DOROTHY WORDSWORTH
(1771-1855)

Floating Island at Hawkshead,
An Incident in the Schemes of Nature

HARMONIOUS POWERS with Nature work
On sky, earth, river, lake, and sea:
Sunshine and storm, whirlwind and breeze
All in one duteous task agree.

Once did I see a slip of earth,
By throbbing waves long undermined,
Loosed from its hold; – how no one knew
But all might see it float, obedient to the wind.

Might see it, from the verdant shore
Dissevered float upon the lake,
Float, with its crest of trees adorned
On which the warbling birds their pastime take.

Food, shelter, safety there they find
There berries ripen, flowerets bloom;
There insects live their lives – and die:
A people world it is; – in size a tiny room.

And thus through many seasons' space
This little island may survive
But Nature, though we mark her not,
Will take away – may cease to give.

Perchance when you are wandering forth
Upon some vacant sunny day
Without an object, hope, or fear,
Thither your eyes may turn – the isle is passed away.

Buried beneath the glittering lake!
Its place no longer to be found,
Yet the lost fragment shall remain,
To fertilize some other ground.

PERCY BYSSHE SHELLEY
(1792-1822)

Ode to the Wild West Wind

I

O WILD West wind, thou breath of Autumn's being,
Thou, from whose unseen presence the leaves dead
Are driven, like ghosts from an enchanter fleeing,

Yellow, and black, and pale, and hectic red,
Pestilence-stricken multitudes: O thou,
Who chariotest to their dark wintry bed

The wingèd seeds, where they lie cold and low,
Each like a corpse within its grave, until
Thine azure sister of the Spring shall blow

Her clarion o'er the dreaming earth, and fill
(Driving sweet buds like flocks to feed in air)
With living hues and odours plain and hill:

Wild spirit, which art moving everywhere;
Destroyer and preserver; hear, oh, hear!

II

Thou on whose stream, mid the steep sky's commotion,
Loose clouds like earth's decaying leaves are shed,
Shook from the tangled boughs of Heaven and Ocean,

Angels of rain and lightning: there are spread
On the blue surface of thine aëry surge,
Like the bright hair uplifted from the head

Of some fierce Mænad, even from the dim verge
Of the horizon to the zenith's height,
The locks of the approaching storm. Thou dirge

Of the dying year, to which this closing night
Will be the dome of a vast sepulchre,
Vaulted with all thy congregated might

Of vapours, from whose solid atmosphere
Black rain, and fire, and hail will burst: oh, hear!

III

Thou who didst waken from his summer dreams
The blue Mediterranean, where he lay,
Lulled by the coil of his crystalline streams,

Beside a pumice isle in Baiæ's bay,

And saw in sleep old palaces and towers
Quivering within the wave's intenser day,

All overgrown with azure moss and flowers
So sweet, the sense faints picturing them! Thou
For whose path the Atlantic's level powers

Cleave themselves into chasms, while far below
The sea blooms and the oozy woods which wear
The sapless foliage of the ocean, know

Thy voice, and suddenly grow gray with fear,
And tremble and despoil themselves; oh, hear!

IV

If I were a dead leaf thou mightest bear;
If I were a swift cloud to fly with thee;
A wave to pant beneath thy power, and share

The impulse of thy strength, only less free
Than thou, O uncontrollable! if even
I were as in my boyhood, and could be

The comrade of thy wanderings over heaven,
As then, when to outstrip thy skiey speed
Scarce seemed a vision; I would ne'er have striven

As thus with thee in prayer in my sore need
Oh, lift me as a wave, a leaf, a cloud!
I fall upon the thorns of life! I bleed!

A heavy weight of hours has chained and bowed
One too like thee: tameless, and swift, and proud.

V

Make me thy lyre, even as the forest is:
What if my leaves are falling like its own!
The tumult of thy mighty harmonies

Will take from both a deep, autumnal tone,
Sweet though in sadness. Be thou, Spirit fierce,
My spirit! Be thou me, impetuous one!

Drive my dead thoughts over the universe
Like withered leaves to quicken a new birth!
And, by the incantation of this verse,

Scatter, as from an unextinguished hearth
Ashes and sparks, my words among mankind!
Be through my lips to unawakened earth

The trumpet of a prophecy! O, Wind,
If Winter comes, can Spring be far behind?

The Cloud

I BRING fresh showers for the thirsting flowers,
  From the seas and the streams;
I bear light shade for the leaves when laid
  In their noonday dreams.
From my wings are shaken the dews that waken
  The sweet buds every one,
When rocked to rest on their mother's breast,
  As she dances about the sun,
I wield the flail of the lashing hail,
  And whiten the green plains under,
And then again I dissolve it in rain,
  And laugh as I pass in thunder.

I sift the snow on the mountains below,
  And their great pines groan aghast;
And all the night 'tis my pillow white,
  While I sleep in the arms of the blast.
Sublime on the towers of my skiey bowers,
  Lightning my pilot sits;
In a cavern under is fettered the thunder,
  It struggles and howls at fits;
Over earth and ocean, with gentle motion,
  This pilot is guiding me,
Lured by the love of the genii that move
 In the depths of the purple sea;

Over the rills, and the crags, and the hills,
    Over the lakes and the plains,
Wherever he dream, under mountain or stream,
        The Spirit he loves remains;
And I all the while bask in Heaven's blue smile,
        Whilst he is dissolving in rains.

The sanguine Sunrise, with his meteor eyes,
        And his burning plumes outspread,
Leaps on the back of my sailing rack,
        When the morning star shines dead;
As on the jag of a mountain crag,
        Which an earthquake rocks and swings,
An eagle alit one moment may sit
        In the light of its golden wings.
And when Sunset may breathe, from the lit sea beneath,
        Its ardours of rest and of love,
And the crimson pall of eve may fall
        From the depth of heaven above,
With wings folded I rest, on mine aëry nest,
        As still as a brooding dove.

That orbèd maiden with white fire laden,
        Whom mortals call the Moon,
Glides glimmering o'er my fleece-like floor,
        By the midnight breezes strewn;
And wherever the beat of her unseen feet,
        Which only the angels hear,

May have broken the woof of my tent's thin roof,
     The stars peep behind her and peer;
And I laugh to see them whirl and flee,
     Like a swarm of golden bees,
When I widen the rent in the wind-built tent,
     Till the calm rivers, lakes, and seas,
Like strips of the sky fallen through me on high,
     Are each paved with the moon and these.

I bind the Sun's throne with a burning zone,
     And the Moon's with a girdle of pearl;
The volcanoes are dim, and the stars reel and swim,
     When the whirlwinds my banner unfurl.
From cape to cape, with a bridge-like shape,
     Over the torrent sea,
Sunbeam-proof, I hang like a roof, –
     The mountains its column be.
The triumphal arch through which I march
     With hurricane, fire, and snow,
When the Powers of the air are chained to my chair,
     Is the million-coloured bow;
The sphere-fire above its soft colours wove,
     While the moist Earth was laughing below.

I am the daughter of Earth and Water,
     And the nursling of the Sky;
I pass through the pores of the ocean and shores;
     I change, but I cannot die.

For after the rain when with never a stain
      The pavilion of Heaven is bare,
And the winds and sunbeams with their convex gleams
      Build up the blue dome of air,
I silently laugh at my own cenotaph,
    And out of the caverns of rain,
Like a child from the womb, like a ghost from the tomb
    I arise and unbuild it again.

from *Orpheus*

AS I have seen
A fierce south blast tear through the darkened sky,
Driving along a rack of winged clouds,
Which may not pause, but ever hurry on,
As their wild shepherd wills them, while the stars,
Twinkling and dim, peep from between the plumes.
Anon the sky is cleared, and the high dome
Of serene heaven, starred with fiery flowers,
Shuts in the shaken earth; or the still moon
Swiftly, yet gracefully, begins her walk,
Rising all bright behind the eastern hills.
I talk of moon, and wind, and stars, and not
Of song; but, would I echo his high song,
Nature must lend me words ne'er used before,
Or I must borrow from her perfect works,
To picture forth his perfect attributes.
He does no longer sit upon his throne
Of rock upon a desert herbless plain,
For the evergreen and knotted ilexes,
And cypresses that seldom wave their boughs,
And sea-green olives with their grateful fruit,
And elms dragging along their twisted veins,
Which drop their berries as they follow fast,
And blackthorn bushes with their infant race
Of blushing rose-blooms; beeches, to lovers dear,

And weeping willow trees; all swift or slow,
As their huge boughs or lighter dress permit,
Have circled in his throne, and Earth herself
Has sent from her maternal breast a growth
Of starlike flowers and herbs of odour sweet,
To pave the temple that his poesy
Has framed, while near his feet grim lions couch,
And kids, fearless from love, creep near his lair.
Even the blind worms seem to feel the sound.
The birds are silent, hanging down their heads,
Perched on the lowest branches of the trees;
Not even the nightingale intrudes a note
In rivalry, but all entranced she listens.

JOHN CLARE
(1793-1864)

A Spring Morning

THE SPRING comes in with all her hues and smells,
In freshness breathing over hills and dells;
O'er woods where May her gorgeous drapery flings,
And meads washed fragrant by their laughing springs.
Fresh are new opened flowers, untouched and free
From the bold rifling of the amorous bee,
The happy time of singing birds is come,
And Love's lone pilgrimage now finds a home;
Among the mossy oaks now coos the dove,
And the hoarse crow finds softer notes for love.
The foxes play around their dens, and bark
In joy's excess, 'mid woodland shadows dark.
The flowers join lips below; the leaves above;
And every sound that meets the ear is Love.

JOHN KEATS
(1795-1821)

To Autumn

I

SEASON OF mists and mellow fruitfulness!
    Close bosom-friend of the maturing sun;
Conspiring with him how to load and bless
    With fruit the vines that round the thatch-eves run;
To bend with apples the moss'd cottage-trees,
    And fill all fruit with ripeness to the core;
        To swell the gourd, and plump the hazel shells
    With a sweet kernel; to set budding more,
And still more, later flowers for the bees,
Until they think warm days will never cease,
        For Summer has o'er-brimmed their clammy cells.

II

Who hath not seen those oft amid thy store?
    Sometimes whoever seeks abroad may find
Thee sitting careless on a granary floor,
    Thy hair soft-lifted by the winnowing wind;
Or on a half-reap'd furrow sound asleep,

Drowsed with the fumes of poppies, while thy hook
    Spares the next swath and all its twined flowers:
And sometimes like a gleaner thou dost keep
   Steady thy laden head across a brook;
   Or by a cyder-press, with patient look,
    Thou watchest the last oozings hours by hours.

III

Where are the songs of Spring? Ay, where are they?
   Think not of them, thou hast thy music too, –
While barred clouds bloom the soft-dying day,
   And touch the stubble-plains with rosy hue;
Then in a wailful choir the small gnats mourn
   Among the river shallows, borne aloft
    Or sinking as the light wind lives or dies;
And full-grown lambs loud bleat from hilly bourn;
   Hedge-crickets sing; and now with treble soft
   The red-breast whistles from a garden-croft;
    And gathering swallows twitter in the skies.

Ode To Psyche

O Goddess! hear these tuneless numbers, wrung
    By sweet enforcement and remembrance dear,
And pardon that thy secrets should be sung
    Even into thine own soft-conched ear:
Surely I dreamt to-day, or did I see
    The winged Psyche with awaken'd eyes?
I wander'd in a forest thoughtlessly,
    And, on the sudden, fainting with surprise,
Saw two fair creatures, couched side by side
    In deepest grass, beneath the whisp'ring roof
    Of leaves and trembled blossoms, where there ran
        A brooklet, scarce espied:

'Mid hush'd, cool-rooted flowers, fragrant-eyed,
    Blue, silver-white, and budded Tyrian,
They lay calm-breathing on the bedded grass;
    Their arms embraced, and their pinions too:
    Their lips touch'd not, but had not bade adieu,
As if disjoined by soft-handed slumber,
And ready still past kisses to outnumber
    At tender eye-dawn of aurorean love:
        The winged boy I knew;
    But who wast thou, O happy, happy dove?
        His Psyche true!

O latest born and loveliest vision far
    Of all Olympus' faded hierarchy!
Fairer than Phoebe's sapphire-region'd star,
Or Vesper, amorous glow-worm of the sky;
Fairer than these, though temple thou hast none,
                    Nor altar heap'd with flowers;
Nor virgin-choir to make delicious moan
                    Upon the midnight hours;
No voice, no lute, no pipe, no incense sweet
    From chain-swung censer teeming;
No shrine, no grove, no oracle, no heat
    Of pale-mouth'd prophet dreaming.

O brightest! though too late for antique vows,
    Too, too late for the fond believing lyre,
When holy were the haunted forest boughs,
    Holy the air, the water, and the fire;
Yet even in these days so far retir'd
    From happy pieties, thy lucent fans,
    Fluttering among the faint Olympians,
I see, and sing, by my own eyes inspir'd.
So let me be thy choir, and make a moan
                    Upon the midnight hours;
Thy voice, thy lute, thy pipe, thy intense sweet
    From swinged censer teeming;
Thy shrine, thy grove, thy oracle, thy heat
    Of pale-mouth'd prophet dreaming.

Yes, I will by thy priest, and build a fane
    In some untrodden region of my mind,
Where branched thoughts, new grown with pleasant
                                        pain,
Instead of pines shall murmur in the wind:
Far, far around shall those dark-cluster'd trees
    Fledge the wild-ridged mountains steep by steep;
And there by zephyrs, streams, and birds, and bees,
    The moss-lain dryads shall be lull'd to sleep;
And in the midst of this wide quietness
    A rosy sanctuary will I dress
With the wreath'd trellis of a working brain,
    With buds, and bells, and stars without a name.
With all the gardener Fancy e'er could feign,
    Who breeding flowers, will never breed the same:
And there shall be for thee all soft delight
    That shadowy thought can win,
A bright torch, and a casement ope at night,
    To let the warm Love in!

On the Grasshopper and the Cricket

The poetry of earth is never dead:
When all the birds are faint with the hot sun,
And hide in cooling trees, a voice will run
From hedge to hedge about the new-mown mead;
That is the Grasshopper's – he takes the lead
In summer luxury, – he has never done
With his delights; for when tired out with fun
He rests at ease beneath some pleasant weed.
The poetry of earth is ceasing never:
On a lone winter evening, when the frost
Has wrought silence, from the stove there shrills
The Cricket's song, in warmth increasing ever,
And seems to one in drowsiness half lost,
The Grasshopper's among some grassy hills.

ELIZABETH BARRETT BROWNING
(1806-1861)

The Best

WHAT'S THE best thing in the world?
June-rose, by May-dew impearl'd;
Sweet south-wind, that means no rain;
Truth, not cruel to a friend;
Pleasure, not in haste to end;
Beauty, not self-deck'd and curl'd
Till its pride is over-plain;
Light, that never makes you wink;
Memory, that gives no pain;
Love, when, so, you're loved again.
What's the best thing in the world?
– Something out of it, I think.

HENRY WADSWORTH LONGFELLOW
(1807-1882)

Snow-Flakes

Out of the bosom of the air,
  Out of the cloud-folds of her garments shaken,
Over the woodlands brown and bare,
  Over the harvest-fields forsaken,
    Silent, and soft, and slow
    Descends the snow.

Even as our clouds fancies take
  Suddenly shape in some divine expression,
Even as the troubled heart doth make
  In the white countenance confession,
    The troubled sky reveals
    The grief it feels.

This is the poem of the air,
  Slowly insilent syllables recorded;
This is the secret despair,
  Long in its cloudy bosom hoarded,
    Now whispered and revealed
    To wood and field.

EMILY BRONTE
(1818-1848)

["Fall, leaves, fall; die, flowers, away"]

FALL, LEAVES, fall; die, flowers, away;
Lengthen night and shorten day;
Every leaf speaks bliss to me
Fluttering from the autumn tree,
I shall smile when wreaths of snow
Blossom where the rose should grow;
I shall sing when night's decay
Ushers in a drearier day.

["Shall earth no more inspire thee"]

SHALL EARTH no more inspire thee,
Thou lonely dreamer now?
Since passion may not fire thee
Shall nature cease to bow?

Thy mind is ever moving
In regions dark to thee;
Recall its useless roving –
Come back and dwell with me.

I know my mountain breezes
Enchant and soothe thee still –
I know my sunshine pleases
Despite thy wayward will.

When day with evening blending
Sinks from the summer sky,
I've seen thy spirit bending
In fond idolatry.

I've watched thee every hour;
I know my mighty sway,
I know my magic power
To drive thy griefs away.

Few hearts to mortals given
On earth so wildly pine;
Yet none would ask a Heaven
More like this Earth than thine.

Then let my winds caress thee;
Thy comrade let me be –
Since nought beside can bless thee,
Return and dwell with me.

["High waving weather"]

HIGH WAVING heather 'neath stormy blasts bending,
Midnight and moonlight and bright shining stars,
Darkness and glory rejoicingly blending,
Earth rising to heaven and heaven descending,
Man's spirit away from its drear dungeon sending,
Bursting the fetters and breaking the bars.

All down the mountain sides wild forests lending
One mighty voice to the life-giving wind,
Rivers their banks in the jubilee rending,
Fast through the valleys a reckless course wending,
Wider and deeper their waters extending,
Leaving a desolate desert behind.

Shining and lowering and swelling and dying,
Changing forever from midnight to noon;
Roaring like thunder, like soft music sighing,
Shadows on shadows advancing and flying,
Lightning-bright flashes the deep gloom defying,
Coming as swiftly and fading as soon.

DORA GREENWELL
(1821-1882)

A Scherzo (A Shy Person's Wishes)

WITH THE wasp at the innermost heart of a peach,
On a sunny wall out of tip-toe reach,
With the trout in the darkest summer pool,
With the fern-seed clinging behind its cool
Smooth frond, in the chink of an aged tree,
In the woodbine's horn with the drunken bee,
With the mouse in its nest in a furrow old,
With the chrysalis wrapt in its gauzy fold;
With things that are hidden, and safe, and bold,
With things that are timid, and shy, and free,
Wishing to be;
With the nut in its shell, with the seed in its pod,
With the corn as it sprouts in the kindly clod,
Far down where the secret of beauty shows
In the bulb of the tulip, before it blows;
With things that are rooted, and form, and deep,
Quiet to lie, and dreamless to sleep;
With things that are chainless, and tameless, and proud,
With the fire in the jagged thunder-cloud,
With the wind in its sleep, with the wind in its waking,

With the drops that go to the rainbow's making,
Wishing to be with the light leaves shaking,
Or stones on some desolate highway breaking;
Far up on the hills, where no foot surprises
The dew as it falls, or the dust as it rises;
To be couched with the beast in its torrid lair,
Or drifting on ice with the polar bear,
With the weaver at work at his quiet loom;
Anywhere, anywhere, out of this room!

EMILY DICKINSON
(1830-1886)

["A Light exists in Spring"]

A LIGHT exists in Spring
Not present on the Year
At any other period –
When March is scarcely here

A Color stands abroad
On Solitary Fields
That Science cannot overtake
But Human Nature feels.

It waits upon the Lawn,
It shows the furthest Tree
Upon the furthest Slope you know
It almost speaks to you.

Then as Horizons step
Or Noons report away
Without the Formula of sound
It passes and we stay –

A quality of loss
Affecting our Content
As Trade had sudenly encroached
Upon a Sacrament.

The Sky is Low

THE SKY is low, the clouds are mean,
A travelling flake of snow
Across a barn or through a rut
Debates if it will go.

A narrow wind complains all day
How someone treated him;
Nature, like us, is sometimes caught
Without her diadem.

"The Lilac is an ancient shrub"

The Lilac is an ancient shrub
But ancienter than that
The firmamental Lilac
Upon the Hill tonight –
The Sun subsiding on his Course
Bequeaths this final Plant
To Contemplation – not to Touch –
The Flower of Occident.
Of one Corolla is the West –
The Calyx is the Earth –
The Capsules burnished Seeds the Stars
The Scientist of Faith
His research has but just begun –
Above his synthesis
The Flora unimpeachable
To Time's Analysis –
"Eye hath not seen" may possibly
Be current with the Blind
But let not Revelation
By theses be detained –

"Exhilaration is the Breeze"

Exhilaration is the Breeze
That lifts us from the Ground
And leaves us in another place
Whose statement is not found –

Returns us not, but after time
We soberly descend
A little newer for the term
Upon Enchanted Ground –

"On this wondrous sea"

On this wondrous sea
Sailing silently,
Ho! Pilot, ho!
Knowest thou the shore
Where no breakers roar –
Where the storm is o'er?

In the peaceful west
Many the sails at rest –
The anchors fast –
Thither I pilot thee –
Land Ho! Eternity!
A shore at last!

THOMAS HARDY
(1840-1928)

A Sign-Seeker

I MARK the months in liveries dank and dry,
    The noontides many-shaped and hued;
     I see the nightfall shades subtrude,
And hear the monotonous hours clang negligently by.

I view the evening bonfires of the sun
    On hills where morning rains have hissed;
     The eyeless countenance of the mist
Pallidly rising when the summer droughts are done.

I have seen the lightning-blade, the leaping star,
    The cauldron of the sea in storm,
     Have felt the earthquake's lifting arm,
And trodden where abysmal fires and snow-cones are.

I learn to prophesy the hid eclipse,
    The coming of eccentric orbs;
     To mete the dust the sky absorbs,
To weigh the sun, and fix the hour each planet dips.

I witness fellow earth-men surge and strive;
   Assemblies meet, and throb, and part;
   Death's sudden finger, sorrow's smart;
– All the vast various moils that mean a world alive.

But that I fain would wot of shuns my sense –
   Those sights of which old prophets tell,
   Those signs the general word so well,
As vouchsafed their unheed, denied my long suspense.

In graveyard green, where his pale dust lies pent
   To glimpse a phantom parent, friend,
   Wearing his smile, and 'Not the end!'
Outbreathing softly: that were blest enlightenment;

Or, if a dead love's lips, whom dreams reveal
   When midnight imps of King Decay
   Delve sly to solve me back to clay,
Should leave some print to prove her spirit-kisses real;

Or, when Earth's Frail lie bleeding of her Strong,
   If some Recorder, as in Writ,
   Near to the weary scene should flit
And drop one plume as pledge that heaven inscrolls the
                                          wrong.

– There are who, rapt to heights of trancelike trust,
   These tokens claim to feel and see,

Read radiant hints of times to be –
Of heart to heart returning after dust to dust.

I Found Her Out There

I FOUND her out there
On a slope few see,
That falls westwardly
To the salt-edged air,
Where the ocean breaks
On the purple strand,
And the hurricane shakes
The solid land.

I brought her here,
And have laid her to rest
In a noiseless nest
No sea beats near.
She will never be stirred
In her loamy cell
By the waves long heard
And loved so well.

So she does not sleep
By those haunted heights
The Atlantic smites
And the blind gales sweep,
Whence she often would gaze
At Dundagel's famed head,
While the dipping blaze

Dyed her face fire-red;

And would sigh at the tale
Of sunk Lyonnesse,
As a wind-tugged tress
Flapped her cheek like a flail:
Or listen at whiles
With a thought-bound brow
To the murmuring miles
She is far from now.

Yet her shade, maybe,
Will creep underground
Till it catch the sound
Of that western sea
As it swells and sobs
Whence she once domiciled,
And joy in its throbs
With the heart of a child.

Where the Picnic Was

WHERE WE made the fire
In the summer time
Of branch and briar
On the hill to the sea,
I slowly climb
Through winter mire,
And scan and trace
The forsaken place
Quite readily.

Now a cold wind blows,
And the grass is gray,
But the spot still shows
As a burnt circle – aye,
And stick-ends charred,
Still strew the sward
Whereon I stand,
Last relic of the band
Who came that day!

Yes, I am here
Just as last year,
And the sea breathes brine
From its strange straight line
Up hither, the same

As when we four came.
– But two have wandered far
From this grassy rise
Into urban roar
Where no picnics are,
And one – has shut her eyes
For evermore.

Growth In May

I enter a daisy-and-buttercup land,
    And thence thread a jungle of grass:
Hurdles and stiles scarce visible stand
    Above the lush stems as I pass.

Hedges peer over, and try to be seen,
    And seem to reveal a dim sense
That amid such ambitious and elbow-high green
    They made a mean show as a fence.

Elsewhere the mead is possessed of neats,
    That range not greatly above
The rich rank thicket which brushes their teats,
    And *her* gown, as she waits for her Love.

The Darkling Thrush

I leant upon a coppice gate
    When Frost was spectre-gray,
And Winter's dregs made desolate
    The weakening eye of day.
The tangled bine-stems scored the sky
    Like strings of broken lyres,
And all mankind that haunted nigh
    Had sought their household fires.

The land's sharp features seemed to be
    The Century's corpse outleant,
His crypt the cloudy canopy,
    The wind his death-lament.
The ancient pulse of germ and birth
    Was shrunken hard and dry,
And every spirit upon earth
    Seemed fervourless as I.

At once a voice arose among
    The bleak twigs overhead
In a full-hearted evensong
    Of joy illimited;
An aged thrush, frail, gaunt, and small,
    In blast-beruffled plume.,
Had chosen thus to fling his soul

Upon the growing gloom.

So little cause for carolings
　　Of such ecstatic sound
Was written on terrestrial things
　　Afar or nigh around,
That I could think there trembled through
　　His happy good-night air
Some blessed Hope, whereof he knew
　　And I was unaware.

LOUISA S. BEVINGTON
(1845-1895?)

Midnight

THERE ARE sea and sky about me,
   And yet nothing sense can mark;
For a mist fills all the midnight
   Adding blindness to the dark.

There is not the faintest echo
   From the life of yesterday:
Not the vaguest stir of foretelling
   Of a narrow on the way.

'Tis negation's hour of triumph
   In the absence of the sun;
'Tis the hour of endings, ended,
   Of beginnings, unbegun.

Yet the voice of awful silence
   Bids my waiting spirit hark;
There is action in the stillness,
   There is progress in the dark.

In the drift of things and forces
   Comes the better from the worse;
Swings the whole of Nature upward,
   Wakes, and thinks – a universe.

There will be more life tomorrow,
   And of life, more life that knows;
Though the sum of force be constant
   Yet the Living ever grows.

So we sing of evolution,
   And step strongly on our ways;
And we live through night in patience,
   And we learn the worth of days.

EDWARD THOMAS
(1878-1917)

Digging

TODAY I think
Only with scents, – scents dead leaves yield,
And bracken, and wild carrot's seed,
And the square mustard field;

Odours that rise
When the spade wounds the root of tree,
Rose, currant, raspberry, or goutweed,
Rhubard or celery;

The smoke's smell, too
Flowing from where a bonfire burns
The dead, the waste, the dangerous,
And all to sweetness turns.

It is enough
To smell, to crumble the dark earth,
While the robin sings over again
Sad songs of Autumn mirth.

The Glory

THE GLORY of the beauty of the morning, –
The cuckoo crying over the untouched dew;
The blackbird that has found it, and the dove
That tempts me on to something sweeter than love;
White clouds ranged even and fair as new-mown hay;
The heat, the stir, the sublime vacancy
Of sky and meadow and forest and my own heart: –
The glory invites me, yet it leaves me scorning
All I can ever do, all I can be,
Beside the lovely motion, shape, and hue,
The happiness I fancy fit to dwell
In beauty's presence. Shall I now this day
Begin to seek as far as heaven, as hell,
Wisdom and strength to match this beauty, start
And tread the pale dust pitted with small dark drops,
In hope to find whatever it is I seek,
Hearkening to short-lived happy-seeming things
That we know naught of, in the hazel copse?
Or must I be content with discontent
As larks and swallows are perhaps with wings?
And shall I ask at the day's end once more
What beauty is, and what I can have meant
By happiness? And shall I let all go,
Glad, weary, or both? Or shall I perhaps know
That I was happy oft and oft before,

✳ 117

Awhile forgetting how I am fast pent,
How dreary-swift, with naught to travel to,
Is Time? I cannot bite the day to the core.

AMY LOWELL
(1874-1925)

Wind and Silver

GREATLY SHINING,
The Autumn moon floats in the thin sky;
And the fish-ponds shake their backs and flash their
dragon
        scales
As she passes over them.

Proportion

IN THE sky there is a moon and stars,
And in my garden there are yellow moths
Fluttering about a white azalea bush.

ELINOR WYLIE
(1885-1928)

Golden Bough

THESE LOVELY groves of fountain-trees that shake
A burning spray against autumnal cool
Descend again in molten drops to make
The rutted path a river and a pool.

They rise in silence, fall in quietude,
Lie still as looking-glass to every sense
Save where their lion-colour in the wood
Roars to miraculous heat and turbulence.

D.H. LAWRENCE
(1885-1930)

Trees in the Garden

AH IN the thunder air
how still the trees are!

And the lime–tree, lovely and tall, every leaf silent
hardly looses even a last breath of perfume.

And the ghostly, creamy coloured little tree of leaves
white, ivory white among the rambling greens
how evanescent, variegated elder, she hesitates on the
green grass
as if, in another moment, she would disappear
with all her grace of foam!

And the larch that is only a column, it goes up too tall to
see:
and the balsam pines that are blue with the grey–blue
blueness of things from the sea,
and the young copper beech, its leaves red–rosy at the
ends
how still they are together, they stand so still

in the thunder air, all strangers to one another
as the great grass glows upwards, strangers in the silent
garden.

from *Craving for Spring*

I WISH it were spring in the world.

Let it be spring!
Come, bubbling, surging tide of sap!
Come, rush of creation!
Come, life! surge through this mass of mortification!
Come, sweep away these exquisite, ghastly first–flowers,
                    which are rather last–flowers!
Come, thaw down their cool portentousness, dissolve
                                them:
snowdrops, straight, death–veined exhalations of white
                    and purple crocuses,
flowers of the penumbra, issue of corruption, nourished
                    in mortification,
jets of exquisite finality;
Come, spring, make havoc of them!
[...]
I want the fine, kindling wine–sap of spring,
gold, and of inconceivably fine, quintessential
                                brightness,
rare almost as beams, yet overwhelmingly potent,
strong like the greatest force of world–balancing.
[...]
I wish it were spring, thundering
delicate, tender spring.

[...]
Oh, in the spring, the bluebell bows him down for very
                                      exuberance,
exulting with secret warm excess
bowed down with his inner magnificence!
[...]
The gush of spring is strong enough
to play with the globe of earth like a ball on a fountain;
At the same time it opens the tiny hands of the hazel
with such infinite patience.
The power of the rising, golden, all–creative sap could
                                      take the earth
and heave it off among the stars, into the invisible;
the same sets the throstle at sunset on a bough
singing against the blackbird;
comes out in the hesitating tremor of the primrose,
and betrays its candour in the round white strawberry
                                      flower,
is dignified in the foxglove, like a Red–Indian brave.

Ah come, come quickly, spring!
Come and lift us towards our culmination, we myriads;
we who have never flowered, like patient cactuses.
Come and lift us to our end, to blossom, bring us to our
                                      summer,
we who are winter–weary in the winter of the world.

Glory

GLORY IS of the sun, too, and the sun of suns,
and down the shafts of his splendid pinions
run tiny rivers of peace.

Most of his time, the tiger pads and slouches in a
                                    burning peace.
And the small hawk high up turns round on the slow
                                    pivot of peace.
Peace comes from behind the sun, with the peregrine
                          falcon, and the owl.
Yet all of these drink blood.

GALLERY OF POETS

Geoffrey Chaucer, 16th century, English School

Sir Thomas Wyatt, by Hans Holbein, 1535-37

Sir Walter Raleigh, by the 'H' Monogrammist, 1588

Sir Philip Sidney, National Portrait Gallery, London

Samuel Daniel

Michael Drayton

William Shakespeare

Robert Herrick

Henry Vaughan

Thomas Phillips, William Blake

William Wordsworth, 1842, National Portrait Gallery, London

Percy Bysshe Shelley

John Clare, by William Hilton, 1820, National Portrait Gallery, London

John Keats

Elizabeth Barrett Browning, by Macaire Havre,1859.

Emily Dickinson

Thomas Hardy

Amy Lowell

D.H. Lawrence

A NOTE
ON NATURE POETRY

Easy to see why there are so many poems written to Spring and Summer. Many of the poems in this collection find their inspiration in the reawakening of the year. In the British pastoral tradition, Spring is the time of rebirth, as symbolized by Easter and Christ's resurrection. Secular poetry, though, celebrates the re-awakening of love, of human, profane, erotic (and heterosexual) love. The fusion of love and Spring, of love and Maytime, flowers, sunshine, is ancient. The British poetic tradition builds on the Greek tradition of bucolic themes. Great early poems of the British Nature tradition include 'Sumer is y-cumen in', that famous hymn to the rebirth of Spring and warmth. The strength of the mediæval rhythms continues today undiminished. It is (partially) the solidity of the poetic rhythm in 'Sumer is y-cumen in' that makes the poem so successful. The rhymes, too, do not jar, as so often in British poetry from the Victorian era onwards. The rhymes of Langland, Chaucer and the mediæval English poets weld their verses together. In Chaucer's poem included here the rhyme scheme is as complex as any in troubadour or French Symbolist poetry, but Chaucer sticks to strong, basic end-words: 'blake', 'make', 'wake' and 'shake'.

Just as beautiful as 'Sumer is y-comen in', though less well known, are the many anonymous poems of Nature, of the mediæval era, of which "Lenten is come with love to towne" is such a delicious example. In Nature poetry, whether of the early mediæval epoch or of contemporary poets, notions of love, Spring, childhood and Paradise fuse. Terms such as Paradise, idyll, Arcadia, Eden and Golden Age are different names for a fount of feeling, to do with love/ Nature/ childhood/ purity, which lies at the heart of Nature poetry.

By the time of the Renaissance, every poet became proficient not only in composing love sonnets, but also of evoking an Arcadian moment. Elizabethan poetry is particularly rich in pastoral or Nature works. All the great names of the Elizabethan era – Spenser, Marlowe, Drayton, Daniel, Shakespeare – produced pastoral verse. One of the most common situations concerned the shepherdess, where the dream of a pre-sinful Paradise, where sheep roam and flutes are hear echoing over the hills, is combined with the earthy delights of erotic love. As with the courtly love poetry tradition, Nature poetry in the Elizabethan age was infused with erotic desire. One can see sublimated or displaced erotic yearning in some of the descriptions of Nature in this collection. In the effusions of the Romantics – Keats, Shelley, Wordsworth and Coleridge – it's easy to spot the erotic qualities.

Nature poetry also takes one back to basics, so that when Keats speaks evocatively of Autumn, it is something that transcends its era, and becomes universal. For Autumn is everywhere. Keats's poem 'To Autumn' might happily apply to Autumn 1022, or 550 BC, or any time between now and the last Ice Age, and back further. If pollution reaches catastrophic levels In the future, autumn as we know it may be severely altered, or it may disappear. Already we are told that over half the trees in Britain are sickly because of human-made pollution. This is a fact that would surely sadden Keats, Wordsworth and the Romantics:

> When Keats wrote of the season of mists and mellow fruitfulness, he was not thinking of August or even early September. But in the age of the motor-car, the British may have to get accustomed to an early autumn.[1]

Among the delights included in this book there is Robert Herrick's magnificent 'The Argument of His Book'. This is a truly majestic fourteen-line poem, an invocation to the Nature, and of humans interacting with Nature. It is, essentially, a list-poem, where the poet lists the things he will sing about in the rest of his book:

> I sing of *Brooks*, of *Blossomes, Birds,* and
> Bowers:
> Of *April, May,* of *June,* and *July*-Flowers.
> I sing of *May-poles, Hock-carts, Wassails,*
> Wakes,

---

1 Geoffrey Lean: "Revealed: why Autumn came early to Britain this year", *The Independent on Sunday*, 11 September 1994, 1

Of *Bride-grooms, Brides*, and of their
                              Bridall-cakes.
I write of *Youth*, of *Love*, and have Accesse
By these, to sing of cleanly-*Wantonesse*.

But Herrick couches his list in simple,
dramatic English, a form of direct, powerful
English that people since Herrick's time have
associated with the Bible. The rest of his poetry
(in his *Hesperides)* followed the plan outlined
in this poem 'The Argument of His Book'.
Herrick was particularly well placed to write
Nature poetry. Like Coleridge, Wordsworth and
Brontë, Herrick lived in the midst of the
countryside – in the relative isolation of Dean
Prior, on the edge of Dartmoor in Devon.
Though at times he fought against his
provincial setting, and hankered after the
civilization of London, one can see the deep
inspiration that the landscape of Devonshire
had for Herrick. For many of the poets included
here Britain (and America) would have been a
much more 'pastoral' landscape than it is in the
20th century. There would have many more
trees, far fewer roads, no cars, planes, trains,
electric lights, pylons, pipes, road signs, and
so on. The landscape that poets such as
Langland, Chaucer, Wyatt, Parnell, Smith, Keats

and Brontë lived in was dramatically different from the urbanized world of the 20th century. There are, of course, continuities between the mediæval and Elizabethan period and now: the same rivers flow, the same birds sing (minus a few species), the same trees rustle their leaves in Autumn. It is (partly) this continuity that makes the poetry of Langland and Sidney and all the other poets collected here so enduring. The relationship with Nature is one of those everlasting relationships that humanity is perpetually dealing with (like the relation to the body, to God, to politics).

Dora Grenwell, who died in 1882, published six volumes of poetry. Her poem 'Scherzo', collected here, does two powerful things. First, it delays the main verb of the single-sentence, so that only right at the end of the poem is the meaning clear. Secondly, it pinpoints one of the fundamental desires of the Nature poet: *to be out there, in Nature*. After listing all sorts of places she'd like to be:

> With the trout in the darkest summer pool,
> With the fern-seed clinging behind its cool
> Smooth frond, in the chink of an aged tree,
> In the woodbine's horn with the drunken
> bee,
> With the mouse in its nest in a furrow old,

With the chrysalis wrapt in its gauzy fold...

She says at the end of the poem: 'Anywhere, anywhere, out of this room!' Many of the poems collected here move from Nature poetry to religious poetry, or, to put it succinctly, from Nature to God. Much of Nature poetry is pantheistic, describing the experience of 'God-in-Nature'. Nature poets write of a spirit or force in the world, and this is identified with God in the Western world. In the East, notions such the Tao or the Gnostic 'One' are equivalents. Elizabeth Barrett Browning's poem 'The Best' (collected here) opens with a wonderful line: 'What's the best thing in the world?' And she lists some of the wonders of Nature (a rose in June, May-dew, the wind, etc), but finally announces:

What's the best thing in the world?
– Something out of it, I think.

It's as if this world can't be exquisitely beautiful on its own. There must be some 'reason' for the beauty, or some creator of it all, which is regarded as God in Western Nature poetry.

One finds archetypal imagery in the Nature

poetry collected here. There is the wood, for example, such a key part of Shakespeare's plays. In Sidney's poem from *The Countess of Pembroke's Arcadia* they are 'the delight of solitariness'. In Thomas Wyatt's "I must go walk the woods so wild", the forest becomes a place of wilderness and banishment (again a common theme in Shakespeare). In Walter Raleigh's 'The Nymph's Reply to the Sheepheard' we find the archetypal (indeed, stereotypical) imagery of the shepherd abroad in the countryside meeting the nymph. By the time of Henry Vaughan's poetry, God and Christianity has infused Nature poetry, so that Nature become subordinated to (part of) God's divine plan. But the fundamental love of Nature continues unabated in Shelley, Long-fellow, Browning, the Wordsworths, up to and beyond Thomas Hardy. During the changes from mediæval God-fearing to Renaissance humanism and Classicism, to Metaphysical God-intoxication to Romantic pantheism and beyond to modern secularization, the passion for Nature is undiminished. Indeed, in the post-1945 era, with the rise of the Green and ecological movements,[2] Nature poetry is alive

---

2 See *Green Voices*, Terry Gifford, Manchester University Press 1995.

and thriving (in Ted Hughes, R.S. Thomas, Peter Redgrove, Seamus Heaney, George Mackay Brown, Sorley Maclean and others.

ARTS, PAINTING, SCULPTURE

web: www.crmoon.com • e-mail: cresmopub@yahoo.co.uk

The Art of Andy Goldsworthy
Andy Goldsworthy: Touching Nature
Andy Goldsworthy in Close-Up
Andy Goldsworthy: Pocket Guide
Andy Goldsworthy In America
Land Art: A Complete Guide
The Art of Richard Long
Richard Long: Pocket Guide
Land Art In Great Britain
Land Art in Close-Up
Land Art In the U.S.A.
Land Art: Pocket Guide
Installation Art in Close-Up
Minimal Art and Artists In the 1960s and After
Colourfield Painting
Land Art DVD, TV documentary
Andy Goldsworthy DVD, TV documentary
The Erotic Object: Sexuality in Sculpture From Prehistory to the Present Day
Sex in Art: Pornography and Pleasure in Painting and Sculpture
Postwar Art
Sacred Gardens: The Garden in Myth, Religion and Art
Glorification: Religious Abstraction in Renaissance and 20th Century Art
Early Netherlandish Painting
Jasper Johns
Brice MardenLeonardo da Vinci
Piero della Francesca
Giovanni Bellini
Fra Angelico: Art and Religion in the Renaissance
Mark Rothko: The Art of Transcendence
Frank Stella: American Abstract Artist
Alison Wilding: The Embrace of Sculpture
Vincent van Gogh: Visionary Landscapes
Eric Gill: Nuptials of God
Constantin Brancusi: Sculpting the Essence of Things
Max Beckmann
Gustave Moreau
Caravaggio
Egon Schiele: Sex and Death In Purple Stockings
Delizioso Fotografico Fervore: Works In Process I
Sacro Cuore: Works In Process 2
The Light Eternal: J.M.W. Turner
The Madonna Glorified: Karen Arthurs

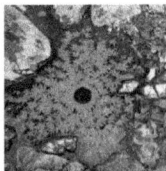

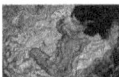

LITERATURE

J.R.R. Tolkien: The Books, The Films, The Whole Cultural Phenomenon
J.R.R. Tolkien: Pocket Guide
Beauties, Beasts and Enchantment: Classic French Fairy Tales
Tolkien's Heroic Quest
Brothers Grimm: German Popular Stories
Sexing Hardy: Thomas Hardy and Feminism
Thomas Hardy's *Tess of the d'Urbervilles*
Thomas Hardy's *Jude the Obscure*
Thomas Hardy: The Tragic Novels
Love and Tragedy: Thomas Hardy
The Poetry of Landscape in Hardy
Wessex Revisited: Thomas Hardy and John Cowper Powys
Wolfgang Iser: Essays and Interviews
Petrarch, Dante and the Troubadours
Maurice Sendak and the Art of Children's Book Illustration
Andrea Dworkin
Cixous, Irigaray, Kristeva: The *Jouissance* of French Feminism
Julia Kristeva: Art, Love, Melancholy, Philosophy, Semiotics and Psychoanalysis
Hélène Cixous I Love You: The *Jouissance* of Writing
Luce Irigaray: Lips, Kissing, and the Politics of Sexual Difference
Peter Redgrove: Here Comes the Flood
Peter Redgrove: Sex-Magic-Poetry-Cornwall
Lawrence Durrell: Between Love and Death, East and West
Love, Culture & Poetry: Lawrence Durrell
Cavafy: Anatomy of a Soul
German Romantic Poetry: Goethe, Novalis, Heine, Hölderlin
Novalis: *Hymns To the Night*
Feminism and Shakespeare
Shakespeare: *The Sonnets*
Shakespeare: Love, Poetry & Magic
The Passion of D.H. Lawrence
D.H. Lawrence: Symbolic Landscapes
D.H. Lawrence: Infinite Sensual Violence
The Ecstasies of John Cowper Powys
Sensualism and Mythology: The Wessex Novels of John Cowper Powys
Amorous Life: John Cowper Powys (H.W. Fawkner)
Postmodern Powys: New Essays on John Cowper Powys (Joe Boulter)
Rethinking Powys: Critical Essays on John Cowper Powys
Paul Bowles & Bernardo Bertolucci
Rainer Maria Rilke
Joseph Conrad: *Heart of Darkness*
In the Dim Void: Samuel Beckett
Samuel Beckett Goes into the Silence
André Gide: Fiction and Fervour
Jackie Collins and the Blockbuster Novel
Blinded By Her Light: The Love-Poetry of Robert Graves

POETRY

Ursula Le Guin: *Walking In Cornwall*
Peter Redgrove: Here Comes The Flood
Peter Redgrove: Sex-Magic-Poetry-Cornwall
Dante: Selections From the *Vita Nuova*
Petrarch, Dante and the Troubadours
William Shakespeare: *The Sonnets*
William Shakespeare: Complete Poems
Blinded By Her Light: The Love-Poetry of Robert Graves
Emily Dickinson: Selected Poems
Emily Brontë: Poems
Thomas Hardy: Selected Poems
Percy Bysshe Shelley: Poems
John Keats: Selected Poems
John Keats: Poems of 1820
D.H. Lawrence: Selected Poems
Edmund Spenser: Poems
Edmund Spenser: *Amoretti*
John Donne: Poems
Henry Vaughan: Poems
Sir Thomas Wyatt: Poems
Robert Herrick: Selected Poems
Rilke: Space, Essence and Angels in the Poetry of Rainer Maria Rilke
Rainer Maria Rilke: Selected Poems
Friedrich Hölderlin: Selected Poems
Arseny Tarkovsky: Selected Poems
Paul Verlaine: Selected Poems
Novalis: *Hymns To the Night*
Arthur Rimbaud: Selected Poems
Arthur Rimbaud: *A Season in Hell*
Arthur Rimbaud and the Magic of Poetry
D.J. Enright: By-Blows
Jeremy Reed: *Brigitte's Blue Heart*
Jeremy Reed: *Claudia Schiffer's Red Shoes*
Gorgeous Little Orpheus
Radiance: New Poems
Crescent Moon Book of Nature Poetry
Crescent Moon Book of Love Poetry
Crescent Moon Book of Mystical Poetry
Crescent Moon Book of Elizabethan Love Poetry
Crescent Moon Book of Metaphysical Poetry
Crescent Moon Book of Romantic Poetry
Pagan America: New American Poetry

J.R.R. Tolkien: The Books, The Films, The Whole Cultural Phenomenon
J.R.R. Tolkien: Pocket Guide
The *Lord of the Rings* Movies: Pocket Guide
The Ghost Dance: The Origins of Religion
The Cinema of Hayao Miyazaki
Hayao Miyazaki: *Princess Mononoke*: Pocket Movie Guide
Hayao Miyazaki: *Spirited Away*: Pocket Movie Guide
The Peyote Cult
HomeGround: The Kate Bush Anthology
Tim Burton : Hallowe'en For Hollywood
Ken Russell
Cixous, Irigaray, Kristeva: The *Jouissance* of French Feminism
Julia Kristeva: Art, Love, Melancholy, Philosophy, Semiotics and Psychoanalysis
Luce Irigaray: Lips, Kissing, and the Politics of Sexual Difference
Hélene Cixous I Love You: The *Jouissance* of Writing
Andrea Dworkin
'Cosmo Woman': The World of Women's Magazines
Women in Pop Music
Discovering the Goddess (Geoffrey Ashe)
The Poetry of Cinema
The Sacred Cinema of Andrei Tarkovsky
Andrei Tarkovsky: Pocket Guide
Andrei Tarkovsky: *Mirror*: Pocket Movie Guide
Walerian Borowczyk: Cinema of Erotic Dreams
Jean-Luc Godard: The Passion of Cinema
Jean-Luc Godard: Pocket Guide
John Hughes and Eighties Cinema
Ferris Buller's Day Off: Pocket Movie Guide
The Cinema of Richard Linklater
Liv Tyler: Star In Ascendance
Blade Runner and the Films of Philip K. Dick
Paul Bowles and Bernardo Bertolucci
Media Hell: Radio, TV and the Press
Detonation Britain: Nuclear War in the UK
Feminism and Shakespeare
Wild Zones: Pornography, Art and Feminism
Sex in Art: Pornography and Pleasure in Painting and Sculpture
Sexing Hardy: Thomas Hardy and Feminism

The Light Eternal is a model monograph, an exemplary job. The subject matter of the book is beautifully organised and dead on beam. (Lawrence Durrell)
It is amazing for me to see my work treated with such passion and respect. (Andrea Dworkin)
Sex-Magic-Poetry-Cornwall is a very rich essay... It is like a brightly-lighted box. (Peter Redgrove)

CRESCENT MOON PUBLISHING P.O. Box 1312, Maidstone, Kent, ME14 5XU, Great Britain
0044-1622-729593 cresmopub@yahoo.co.uk www.crmoon.com

www.ingramcontent.com/pod-product-compliance
Lightning Source LLC
Chambersburg PA
CBHW060015050426
42448CB00012B/2757